RACIAL JUSTICE!

What Is the

BLACK LIVES MATTER MOVEMENT?

HEDREICH NICHOLS WITH KELISA WING

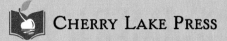
CHERRY LAKE PRESS

Published in the United States of America by Cherry Lake Publishing Group
Ann Arbor, Michigan
www.cherrylakepublishing.com

Reading Adviser: Marla Conn, MS, Ed., Literacy specialist, Read-Ability, Inc.
Content Adviser: Kelisa Wing
Book Design: Felicia Macheske

Photo Credits: © artshock/Shutterstock.com, cover, 1, 4, 5; © Ira Bostic/Shutterstock.com, 5; © Rena Schild/Shutterstock.com, 6; © lev radin/Shutterstock.com, 7; Library of Congress/Photograph by Russell Lee, LOC Control No.: 2017740552, 9; Library of Congress/LOC Control No.: 2017679761, 11; Library of Congress/LOC Control No.: 2007664640, 12; © Grindstone Media Group/Shutterstock.com, 15; © ADLC/Shutterstock.com, 16; © Hung Chung Chih/Shutterstock.com, 19; © Audley C Bullock/Shutterstock.com, 21; © Karl Tapales/Shutterstock.com, 23; © Sylvia Buchholz/REUTERS/Alamy, 24; © Allison C Bailey/Shutterstock.com, 25; © Cultura Motion/Shutterstock.com, 27; © trevorwk/Shutterstock.com, 29

Graphics Throughout: © debra hughes/Shutterstock.com; © GoodStudio/Shutterstock.com; © Natewimon Nantiwat/Shutterstock.com; © Galyna_P/Shutterstock.com

Library of Congress Cataloging-in-Publication Data

Names: Nichols, Hedreich, author. | Wing, Kelisa, author.
Title: What is the Black Lives Matter movement? / Hedreich Nichols, Kelisa Wing.
Description: Ann Arbor, Michigan : Cherry Lake Publishing, [2021] |
   Series: Racial justice in America | Includes index. | Audience: Grades 4-6 | Summary: "Race in America has been avoided in children's education for too long.'What Is the Black Lives Matter Movement?' explores the goals and history of the movement in a comprehensive, honest, and age-appropriate way. Developed in conjunction with educator, advocate, and author Kelisa Wing to reach children of   all races and encourage them to approach race issues with open eyes and minds. Includes 21st Century Skills and   content, as well as a PBL activity across the Racial Justice in America series. Also includes a table of contents, glossary,   index, author biography, sidebars, educational matter, and activities"— Provided by publisher.
Identifiers: LCCN 2020040008 (print) | LCCN 2020040009 (ebook) | ISBN 9781534180222 (hardcover) | ISBN 9781534181939 (paperback) | ISBN 9781534181236 (pdf) | ISBN 9781534182943 (ebook)
Subjects: LCSH: Black lives matter movement--Juvenile literature. | African Americans—Civil rights—Juvenile   literature. | United States—Race relations—Juvenile literature. | Racial profiling in law enforcement—United States—Juvenile literature. | African Americans—Social conditions—21st century—Juvenile literature. | Racism—United States—Juvenile literature.
Classification: LCC E185.86 .N53 2021 (print) | LCC E185.86 (ebook) | DDC 323.1196/073--dc23
LC record available at https://lccn.loc.gov/2020040008
LC ebook record available at https://lccn.loc.gov/2020040009

Cherry Lake Publishing Group would like to acknowledge the work of the Partnership for 21st Century Learning, a Network of Battelle for Kids. Please visit http://www.battelleforkids.org/networks/p21 for more information.

Printed in the United States of America
Corporate Graphics

Many thanks to Tina, Aunt Jean, Bonnie, Auntie Barbara, and my Swiss family.

Hedreich Nichols, author, educator, and host of the YouTube series on equity #SmallBites, retired Grammy-nominated singer-songwriter turned EdTech teacher who uses her experience as a "one Black friend" to help others understand race, equity, and how to celebrate diversity. When not educating and advocating, she enjoys making music with her son, multi-instrumentalist @SwissChrisOnBass.

Kelisa Wing honorably served in the U.S. Army and has been an educator for 14 years. She is the author of *Promises and Possibilities: Dismantling the School to Prison Pipeline*, *If I Could: Lessons for Navigating an Unjust World*, and *Weeds & Seeds: How to Stay Positive in the Midst of Life's Storms*. She speaks both nationally and internationally about discipline reform, equity, and student engagement. Kelisa lives in Northern Virginia with her husband and two children.

CHAPTER 1

An Intro to Black Lives Matter

Almost everyone is treated unfairly at some time in their life. People can be treated poorly because they belong to a certain cultural group or because of what they stand for. They can be discriminated against because of mental or physical disabilities. People can be treated unfairly because they are too rich or too poor, too tall or too short, too loud or too quiet, too religious or not religious enough.

But unfairness and anti-Black racism are different. America's legal and educational systems make it harder for people in the Black community to get a good education, be successful, and build wealth. When these systems put one cultural group at a disadvantage, it's called systemic racism.

Black people are also subject to racial profiling. In 2012, Trayvon Martin was killed by a Neighborhood Watch volunteer. The Black teenager was unarmed and "looked suspicious." The shooter was charged with murder but found not guilty. This made people angry and sad. Alicia Garza, Patrisse Cullors, and Opal Tometi called for justice for Trayvon using the hashtag #BlackLivesMatter. The Black Lives Matter (BLM) movement was born the next year.

Protesters rally toward the Sanford Police department in support

In 2014, another unarmed teenager, Michael Brown, was murdered by police in Ferguson, Missouri. Again, BLM responded, launching the organization into the mainstream as a movement. Since then, those advocating for justice in the deaths of other Black people have used the hashtag #BlackLivesMatter. The words "Black lives matter" are another way of saying, "Hey, the lives of Black people are important too!"

Signs in front of the White House show support for the Black Lives Matter movement in 2020.

THIS WAS NOT A
WAKE-UP CAL
THIS WAS THE
LAST STRA

BLM supports communities in their fight against anti-Black racism. It also supports efforts by other marginalized groups—women's rights, LGBTQ (lesbian, gay, bisexual, transgender, and queer) rights, and immigrants' legal and human rights. Understanding the Black Lives Matter movement can help you support people who experience racism and the loss of human rights.

Bill De Blasio, Al Sharpton, and volunteers paint a Black Lives Matter mural on Fifth Avenue in New York City, in 2020.

CHAPTER 2

Backstory

Slavery in America started before the framing of the country's legal system. George Washington, James Madison, Benjamin Franklin, and others had enslaved people working in their homes cooking and cleaning. The enslaved Africans and their descendants worked the land of their enslavers to plant and harvest.

People rich enough to own people as slaves usually got richer because they kept the money they would have had to pay regular workers. The enslavers also had more rights and more privileges. People in slavery got nothing. They could not earn money. They could not inherit money from their fathers or pass money on to their children, which is how White families have been able to gain wealth across generations. For most of the Black people in America, especially in the South, enslavement continued for almost 250 years, from 1619 to 1865.

Once slaves were free, they lived in poverty and many died. If they survived, another 100 years of Jim Crow laws and segregation made America a difficult place for most former slaves and their descendants. These laws made it legal in many instances to prevent Black people from owning land or businesses.

Segregation was everywhere in American until the late 1900s. Its effects are still felt today.

There were exceptions, like Harlem, New York, and "Black Wall Street" in Tulsa, Oklahoma. These Black communities flourished with their own stores, banks, restaurants, luxury hotels, and fine homes. Black achievement drew many to these growing communities, but it also produced resentment in surrounding White communities. Black residents often faced violence and terrorism by White people, who beat and killed them and burned their homes and businesses to the ground.

Black Wall Street was a wealthy Black community that flourished in the early 1900s. O. W. Gurley was a teacher, politician, and landowner. He mapped out a community he called Greenwood. Black people seeking opportunity came to Greenwood and built successful businesses. Greenwood became one of the most prominent and wealthy post-**emancipation** communities in the country.

In 1921, a Black man of Greenwood was accused of a crime against a White woman. A White mob demanded the man be handed over to them. Fearing a lynching, a large group of armed Black men arrived to protect him. White citizens responded by burning Greenwood down using torches and kerosene bombs dropped from airplanes. The angry mob completely destroyed the 35-square-block community, killing hundreds. No one was ever **prosecuted** for the destruction of Black Wall Street.

Lynching is a word that describes illegal mob killings of Black people. White people would forcibly take Black people and hang them from trees, burn them alive, or beat them until death or near death. Lynching was used to control and terrorize the Black community, and often it happened in front of an audience. Learn more about the history of lynching from the Smithsonian film *An Outrage*.

Greenwood after the destruction of the mobs in 1921.

NAACP Meeting, Atlanta, Georgia, June 1, 1920.

Although slavery had ended, equal rights were not given to Black citizens. Especially in the South, segregation, violence, and lynching were used to maintain the pre–Civil War social order in which White people maintained power over Black people.

To combat violence and discrimination, organizations like the National Association for the Advancement of Colored People (NAACP) were formed. Founded in 1909, the NAACP is the oldest, perhaps most well-known organization fighting for civil rights. Much like today's BLM movement, it began in response to riots in which Black people were targeted and killed. Most of the NAACP's early leadership was White and included women suffragists like Mary White Ovington and Inez Milholland.

Later in the 1900s, came the Congress of Racial Equality, the Southern Christian Leadership Conference (SCLC, led by Dr. Martin Luther King), and the Student Non-Violent Coordinating Committee (founded by Inez Baker).

These activist groups became the driving forces behind the great civil rights movement of the 1960s. Protests highlighted the systemic injustices still endured by Black people 100 years after the end of slavery. Activists led the Black community in advocating for human rights and for legal help and protections that had been historically denied them. Because of the civil rights movement, schools and businesses began to be integrated. Additionally, laws were made to protect Black people from vigilante and police violence.

CHAPTER 3

BLM Today

After the protests of the 1960s, it seemed that there was real change in issues surrounding race in America. But data collected in the decades that followed showed racial progress in education and jobs had stalled or stopped.

Although the NAACP, SCLC, and other groups never stopped advocating for change, the number of large demonstrations and marches decreased until the 2000s. A number of high-profile killings of Black citizens in police custody and by White vigilantes showed that there was a renewed need for organized protests and anti-racist activism.

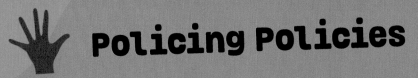

Policing Policies

The majority of police officers today take the job to serve and protect. But cell phone cameras have shined a light on officers who abuse their power. After repeated viral video footage of police violence against Black people, lawmakers have begun to examine policies. The hashtag #BlackLivesMatter is used to call attention to such inequities and advocate for more in-depth investigation and legal reform.

Police and activists collide in downtown Houston, Texas, during protests of the beating and killing of George Floyd by Minneapolis police in May of 2020.

Patrisse Cullors grew up understanding the importance of powerful organizations like the NAACP and the National Action Network. But she didn't feel they were speaking to her generation. With well-known female and LGBTQ leaders, Black Lives Matter speaks to younger citizens. The movement is guided by an alliance of 16 local chapters that have the freedom to act in their communities. BLM's focus is on community action and social justice in the form of the following:

- Directing funding formerly dedicated to policing into educational and community programming.

- Expanding investment in Black business, health care, education, and community ventures to make up for the years Black citizens were kept from accessing and building wealth.

- Ending unfair practices like gerrymandering and voter supression.

Massive crowds on Sunset Boulevard during Black Lives Matter protests. Los Angeles, June 14, 2020.

Deep Dive into Fake News

The First Amendment of the U.S. Constitution guarantees the right to free speech. But how can you tell if what you hear or read is speaking the truth? If you're unsure, go to Factcheck.org, Politifact.org, or Snopes.com. These sites can help you decide if something is true or false. Or print out this worksheet, "How to Identify Fake News in 10 Steps," at *http://library.pfeiffer.edu/Fake-News-Worksheet.pdf* and see if you can figure it out yourself.

The hashtag #SayTheirNames has also been used to call attention to racial injustice that often surrounds the violent deaths of Black people. The website *Sayevery.name* examines the circumstances surrounding the deaths and the outcomes of the legal cases. And mostly, it pays respect to lives ended too soon.

What happens when protests end? Do research online to find out how BLM is making an impact in the fight against racism and discrimination.

The Black Lives Matter movement gained international support when George Floyd was killed by a police officer in 2020. BLM protests began in Minneapolis, where Floyd was murdered, and quickly spread throughout the country. Most major U.S. cities held rallies and marches.

Black Lives Matter protest in Breda, the Netherlands, 2020.

The horrific images of Floyd's murder went viral, and the movement became one of the largest in history. People around the world began to advocate for anti-racist policing and human rights for Black American citizens. They examined racism in their own countries. BLM marches, rallies, and vigils were held in over 60 countries and on every continent except Antarctica. Protests were held in streets, town squares, and in front of U.S. embassies.

Some governments—like those in Fort Worth, Texas, and Washington, D.C.—allowed citizens to paint "Black Lives Matter" on certain streets. The murals, in bold yellow and black letters, cover several city blocks. The mural in Washington, D.C., is near the White House and is large enough to be seen from space.

In the spring, summer, and fall of 2020, an estimated 20 million people protested in support of Black Lives Matter.

Aerial shot of a Black Lives Matter mural on Fulton Street in Brooklyn, New York. It is 375 feet (114.3 meters) wide, and the letters are 28 feet (8.5 m) tall.

In keeping with the movement's values, almost all of the protests worldwide were peaceful. However, some of the protesters were not members of the movement and did not have the same values. Fringe groups looted and vandalized property.

Some media outlets began to focus on violent clashes between citizens and police. Propaganda on social media blamed Black Lives Matter for the violence. Some people wrongly believed that BLM thought only Black lives mattered. They condemned BLM as violent and anti-White. These groups, some with ties to White supremacist groups, started using hashtags like #AllLivesMatter and #BlueLivesMatter.

Tweets by U.S. President Donald Trump also spread anti-BLM sentiment, calling the movement a "symbol of hate." Social media posts and misinformation further inflamed tensions.

Federal troops were sent into some cities to crack down on local protesters. Violent clashes worsened.

When using social media and reading online news, be sure you know the information is from a credible source before believing or sharing it.

Anti-racist groups like #WallofMoms and #WallofVets came out in support of BLM. These largely White groups protested the presence of federal troops and police violence. Local governments filed lawsuits against the U.S. government for violating First Amendment rights. The United Nations and Amnesty International, two government watchdogs, issued human rights violation warnings to the U.S. government because citizens and journalists were being harmed and jailed.

Women dressed in yellow form a "wall of moms" during a march against the death of Elijah McClain and racial injustice in Aurora, Colorado.

Federal troops were withdrawn, but negative media coverage hurt the Black Lives Matter image. Leaders of the movement condemned violence, breaking with groups that weren't focused solely on the issues. Calls for peace and focus on the movement's message have followed.

Military veterans holding a sign and American flag in support of Black lives and First Amendment rights.

DO THE WORK!

ESSENTIAL QUESTION

How can we be anti-racist?

Becoming anti-racist requires actively working against racism using words and actions. This project-based learning assignment will allow you to practice these skills. Read all the books in the *Racial Justice in America* series. Through each "DO THE WORK!" activity, you will research and put together parts of a larger project that will allow you to grow and help others grow as well.

How does civil disobedience play a role in the movement? The Black Lives Matter movement is similar to other movements in the 1960s with its commitment to nonviolence. For this portion of the assignment, research two other movements that utilized civil disobedience and other forms of nonviolent protests. What does the term civil disobedience mean? Why is it effective? What do the movements you researched have in common with BLM? How are they different?

For the presentation of your final work, you can create a collage, magazine, podcast, jigsaw puzzle, poem, video, or social media campaign—anything to demonstrate your learning. No matter what you do, just be creative, learn something new, and publicize your work!

CHAPTER 4

Supporting BLM

There are many ways to support the Black Lives Matter movement. Some people march. Some promote content highlighting the ongoing need for social change on social media. Others help paint murals like the ones pictured in this book. Some people donate to the Black Lives Matter Global Foundation to help fund advocacy groups. Still others support the movement's core values by standing up for Black people or anyone being treated unfairly because of how they look or identify.

Supporting and valuing the lives of Black citizens is supporting and valuing human life. Valuing human life is what Black Lives Matter is all about.

Marching is just one way to show support of the Black
Lives Matter movement.

What can you do to create a safe space to talk about race?

Project ENGAGE

Does your school have a safe space to work through issues of race, identity, and acceptance? How can you apply the core principles of the Black Lives Matter movement to create a more **inclusive** school community, even if no Black people attend your school?

Start a club to talk about racism and anti-racism. Practice civil disagreement, uncomfortable conversation, and agreeing to disagree. On the next page is a structure you can use to get started. Or you can create your own. The important thing is that you find a way to create a more equitable, inclusive world.

E EDUCATE yourself by reading fiction and nonfiction books or articles from diverse authors.

N NAME your feelings about people who are different from you. Do you have biases against certain groups? How did they develop?

G GET rid of biases by working through your feelings. Read about how others have overcome their biases. Or talk to a friend who can help you grow.

A ACTIVELY read and research to learn the stories of people who are different from you.

G GET to know people as individuals. Refuse to generalize.

E ESTABLISH regular meet-ups to talk about and work through issues of race and social justice in your community.

EXTEND YOUR LEARNING

Black Lives Matter. *https://blacklivesmatter.com*

Markovics, Joyce. *2020 Black Lives Matter Marches*. Ann Arbor, MI: Cherry Lake Publishing, 2021

Memory, Jelani. *A Kids Book About Racism*. Portland, OR: A Kids Book About, 2019

Thomas, Angie. *The Hate U Give*. New York, NY: Balzer + Bray, 2017

GLOSSARY

advocating (AD-voh-kay-ting) supporting an idea or a plan

alliance (uh-LYE-uhns) an agreement to work together for some result

civil rights (SIV-uhl RITES) the rights everyone should have to freedom and equal treatment under the law, regardless of who they are

discriminated (dis-krim-uh-NAY-ted) treated unfairly based on differences in such things as race, age, or gender

emancipation (ih-man-suh-PAY-shuhn) the freeing of a person or group from slavery or control

embassies (EM-buh-seez) official places in foreign countries where another government's top person goes to represent their country

gerrymandering (JER-ee-man-dur-ing) drawing lines in voting district maps to favor one group and hurt another

inclusive (in-KLOO-siv) welcoming to everyone

integrated (IN-tuh-gray-tid) not separated by race

Jim Crow (JIHM KROH) the deeply unfair treatment of Black people in the United States through laws that kept them separate from Whites

marginalized (MAHR-jin-ah-lyzd) excluded from power or importance in society

profiling (PROH-file-ing) the act of suspecting or targeting a person based on their mannerisms, dress, or looks

propaganda (prah-puh-GAN-duh) misleading information that is spread to influence the way people think, gain supporters, or damage an opposing group

prosecuted (PRAH-sih-kyoot-id) carried out a legal action in a court of law against a person accused of a crime

racism (RAY-siz-uhm) unfair treatment of people based on the belief that one race is better than another race

segregation (seg-rih-GAY-shuhn) the practice of keeping people or groups apart

systemic (sis-TEM-ik) affecting the entire social, economic, or political world

vigilante (vij-uh-LAN-tee) a person who illegally tries to prevent or punish real or imagined crimes

vigils (VIJ-uhlz) the acts of staying awake at night in order to protest

INDEX